Presented to

_____

On the occasion of

_____

From

_____

Date

_____

LIFE
101

Basics for Life

Colleen L. Reece
& Julie Reece

BARBOUR
PUBLISHING, INC.
Uhrichsville, Ohio

Published by Barbour Publishing, Inc.
P.O. Box 719
Uhrichsville, Ohio 44683
http://www.barbourbooks.com

 Member of the
Evangelical Christian
Publishers Association

Printed in Hong Kong.

LIFE 101

Part 1

LIFE'S LITTLE LESSONS

*Things they never told you you'd need to know
(or maybe you just weren't listening).*

*Show me your ways,
O LORD,
teach me your paths;
guide me in your truth
and teach me,
for you are God
my Savior.*
PSALM 25:4–5

LIFE 101

Move on,
but Don't Slam the Door Behind You

ONE WAY

Jack breathed a sigh of relief on the last day of the part-time job he had held to help pay his way through college. His brand-new degree meant the opportunity for a more prestigious, higher-paying position.

"We can always use you," Jack's supervisor said.

No way will I be back, Jack thought. He didn't want to be rude, so he just smiled—one of the wisest decisions of his life. He discovered jobs were scarce in his chosen field and the bills kept coming in. Part-time work at his former place of employment brought in a small, but steady paycheck until Jack found a job where he could better use his education and experience.

Smile at little kids in grocery carts.
Once upon a time, you were one of them.

Make your bed when you get up,
so if you have visitors,
you won't have to make excuses.

Exercise the first thing in the morning.
It will get you going and you won't have to worry
about it the rest of the day.

If your clothes aren't dirty when you take them
off, hang them up so they won't pile up.

Treat your body well now.
The things you do or don't do today
will affect you
for the rest of your life.

LIFE 101

All About Food

✓ Turn pickle and mustard jars, etc. upside down in hot water to loosen caps.

✓ Toss a couple of soda crackers in your brown and granulated white sugar containers to keep the sugar from hardening.

✓ Plan to cook your meals backwards—write down how long it will take each item to cook.

✓ Remember: two items do *not* usually cook well together in the oven. Figure out when to begin preparing each item to finish the meal on time.

✓ Tally on a piece of paper the number of cups, half cups, tablespoons, and so on listed in a recipe as you add them. If you're distracted while counting, you won't ruin your recipe.

✓ Break eggs into a separate dish before adding. It saves time picking out shells if you goof and saves expensive ingredients if it's a bad egg.

Part 2

STUDY PARTNERS

The difference between pass and fail.

Gather the people together. . .
that they may learn. . . .
<small>DEUTERONOMY 31:12</small>

LIFE 101

*How good and pleasant it is when
brothers live together in unity!*
PSALM 133:1

*Then make my joy complete by
being like-minded, having the same love,
being one in spirit and purpose.
Do nothing out of
selfish ambition or vain conceit,
but in humility consider others
better than yourselves.*
PHILIPPIANS 2:2–3

Live by the Rules

Before you make a move on your best friend's boy-friend or girlfriend, consider this:

✓ You'll lose at least one friend, maybe more.

✓ If you fail, you'll feel ridiculous.

✓ If the person is fickle enough to leave your friend, chances are he or she won't stay with you, either.

✓ Using underhanded means makes you a loser, even if you win.

> Don't date anyone
> who doesn't have
> the qualities
> you are looking for
> in a marriage partner.

LIFE 101

Driving Brian Crazy!

Brian couldn't look at his roommate without gritting his teeth. Dustin's habits and comments ranged from annoying to totally offensive. If Brian had to sit through one more meal watching Dustin chew his dinner with an open mouth, or explain to one more date that the dirty socks and dishes in the living room weren't his, he was going to strangle Dustin.

One day a sentence from something Brian read stuck in his mind. *If you serve someone, it will change your own attitude.* "The person who wrote that didn't have to smell Dustin's socks," Brian muttered. "But if I don't do something, I'll go nuts. I guess it can't do any harm."

He found a card, scribbled, "Hope you do well on your test," pinned it to Dustin's pillow (which he found in the midst of his roommate's dirty-clothes pile) and left for class.

Hours later Brian returned to the empty apartment. A plate of chocolate cookies and a "thinking of you" card lay on his bed.

Change came. Not so much in Dustin—although he did grow more pleasant and made an effort to keep the apartment livable—but mostly in Brian's perception. Several years later, he received a card from the roommate who had almost driven him crazy. It spoke of how important Brian's friendship was to Dustin. The note ended, "You touched my life in more ways than you will ever know. I just want to say, you would be proud of what I am today."

Brian stared at the message, thankful that he hadn't missed knowing Dustin simply because of his dirty socks *and* Brian's unwillingness to look for the good in his friend.

> *. . .pray for them*
> *which despitefully use you. . .*
> MATTHEW 5:44 KJV

13

LIFE 101

No Instant Answers

Kathy got in with the wrong crowd during high school, simply because she was so lonely. She involved herself in drugs, alcohol, and crime, feeling accepted by others who did the same. Eventually, she bottomed out, unable to stand what she'd become.

Kathy decided enough was enough. She had to break her bad habits and move on. When she tried to do this, she discovered she was more isolated than ever. She bitterly told her mother, "I thought when I started making good choices things would be better. They aren't. At least when I was doing all those things I had friends. Now I don't have anyone."

Her mother quietly said, "Kathy, you have the mistaken impression that you can go from a bad crowd to a good crowd overnight. It's just not going to happen. There are no instant answers. I promise you, if you hang on and continue to make good choices, people will start to see and like the new you. You'll make good friends who will value your new standards and you will never have to go through this again."

It wasn't easy and it took a long time, but with the help of God and her family, Kathy hung in there until she found friends, happiness, and freedom.

Part 3

SCHOOL OF
HARD KNOCKS

Learning from life's painful lessons.

When you get to the end
of your rope,
tie a knot and hang on.

LIFE 101

Running Away Versus Breaking Away

There's a time to break away from your family to attend college, get married, or pursue a dream. An eighteen-year-old with a great chance for an out-of-state job is a lot different from a fourteen-year-old who runs away because she thinks her brother gets all the attention. Ecclesiastes 3 says God has a time for everything. It's like a basketball game. Sometimes you race down the floor. Sometimes you pass or play defense. The coach calls the signals.

Off the court, you call your own plays. Seeking the guidance of the Holy Spirit can help you know those plays are not only right for you, but perfectly timed.

When you feel like running, consider the following.

✓ Put things in perspective. What seems horrible at 2:00 A.M. seldom seems so bad the next morning.

✓ Run away if you must, but to the beach, a park, or the library—a quiet place where you can have a few hours to think.

✓ Temporary isolation. Wounded animals often hole up in a cave or den, but only for a time. If they don't come out, they die. You can die physically, emotionally, or spiritually if you isolate yourself too long.

✓ Counseling or support groups. They really do help.

✓ You are important. What if you didn't exist? Picture your family and friends. How would their lives be different? God created you as a special person whose life will touch many others. He expects you to handle tough times with His help and He understands your pain. Remember: He gave His only Son so that we could be free from sin.

LIFE 101

Death by Embarrassment

Contrary to popular belief, no one ever died of embarrassment. Just ask Beth.

"I came close," she relates. "I'd waited forever for Rick to ask me out. He finally did. I had so many butterflies I couldn't eat dinner. I didn't want my stomach to growl, so I grabbed a huge spoonful of peanut butter and ate it before brushing my teeth."

She grimaces. "Mistake number one. Peanut butter and butterflies don't mix. I ended up burping like an overstuffed baby! Rick showed up and walked me to the Jeep. I managed to hold off until he put me in and shut the door, then I let it fly. What a relief! It rocked Rick's Jeep, but he didn't seem to notice."

Beth giggles. "Some relief. He slid in behind the wheel, glanced in the backseat and said, 'Ready, everyone?' "

"Everyone? I cringed. Rick hadn't told me we were double dating. It's funny now, but when it happened, I thought I'd die." Laughter spills over. "The only good thing was I felt so embarrassed I didn't burp again for a week."

LIFE 101

Part 4

READING,
WRITING,
ARITHMETIC

And you thought school was over!

*Study to show yourself
approved unto God. . .*
2 TIMOTHY 2:15 (paraphrased)

LIFE
101

Recommended Reading
*Books I Wish Someone Had Told Me
to Read a Long Time Ago*

Books that Inspire

The Bible

America
Charles Kuralt

Chicken Soup for the Soul
Jack Canfield and Mark Victor Hansen

Diary of Anne Frank

Five Centuries of Verse

God's Smuggler
Brother Andrew

In His Steps
Charles M. Sheldon

Leaves of Gold
edited by Clyde Francis Lytle

LIFE
101

My Utmost for His Highest
Oswald Chambers

The Hiding Place
Corrie ten Boom

The Pursuit of Holiness
Jerry Bridges

Books that Provide
Insight and Direction

The Bible

Man's Search for Meaning
Viktor Frankl

Hinds' Feet on High Places
Hannah Hurnard

The Pilgrim's Progress
John Bunyan

Knowing God
J. I. Packer

Mere Christianity

21

LIFE 101

C. S. Lewis

Practical Guidance for Living Everyday Life

The Bible

A General Legal Guide
A Simplified Guide to Tax Return Preparation

Consumer Reports (before buying anything)

NADA Official Used Car Guide and
The Kelley Blue Book (before buying a car)

What Color Is Your Parachute?

The Book of Virtues
William Bennett

The Elements of Style
Strunk and White

God's Little Instruction Book

Writing

*Here's a road map to help you find
and get where you're going.*

Answer the following questions as honestly as you can. Go back in six months or a year and do the questions again. Compare the answers to see how you're doing.

1. Who am I? Whom do I want to become? Why?

2. What are the five most important things in my life today? Why?

3. What do I believe will be the most important things in my life? Why?

4. Where do I see myself in five, twenty, fifty years?

5. How am I making the world a better place right now? How will I make the world a better place in the future? When will I start?

"For I know the plans I have for you," declares the Lord, "plans to prosper you and not to harm you, plans to give you hope and a future."
JEREMIAH 29:11

LIFE 101

Arithmetic

✓ God + one = a majority.

✓ Everyone is equal in God's eyes.

✓ In marriage, one + one = one.

✓ Spending more money than you earn just doesn't add up.

✓ It's hard to erase first impressions.

✓ Second thoughts are often best.

✓ A little humor in any equation makes things work out better.

✓ If you haven't tried three different ways to accomplish the same thing, don't give up.

✓ If you put God first and others second, you will find happiness.

✓ Spending effort and energy today = success tomorrow.

LIFE
101

Part 5

SUNDAY SCHOOL
LESSONS

Spiritual guidance for every day of the week.

Day 1: *From Grief to Hope*

Weeping may endure for a night,
but joy cometh in the morning.
PSALM 30:5 KJV

Mary and her sister Martha anxiously waited for
Jesus to come. Surely He would heal their brother,
whom He loved, when He had healed so many others! Jesus did not come and Lazarus died. The sisters
sadly prepared him for burial, hot tears falling on

25

the linen wrappings. They laid him to rest in a cave, rolled a stone before it, and the household went into mourning.

"Jesus could have saved Lazarus," Martha said.

"I know." Her sister sighed, eyes filled with sadness.

Four days later Jesus came. Mary and Martha cried, "Lord, if You had been here, our brother would not have died!"

Jesus wept. Then he ordered that the stone be taken from the mouth of the cave. He looked toward heaven and prayed, "Father, I thank You that You have heard me." In a loud voice, he cried, "Lazarus, come forth!"

Torn between grief and hope, the sisters could hardly force themselves to look. A moment later they fell to their knees. Their brother stood before them, alive and smiling. (Based on John 11.)

Even when things seem the darkest, we can
be hopeful Christ will make them better soon.

Day 2: *From Guilt to Forgiveness*

LIFE 101

Though your sins are like scarlet,
they shall be as white as snow.
ISAIAH 1:18

"Master, this woman was taken in adultery. Moses has commanded us that such should be stoned. What do you say?"

The accused woman cringed, her whole miserable life flashing before her. She waited for Jesus to give His assent. Instead, He stooped down. She saw Him write on the ground with his finger. Was it her death sentence?

The crowd demanded that Jesus reply. He said, "He that is without sin among you, let him first cast a stone at her."

The woman scarcely dared breathe. She waited for the first sharp stone to tear her flesh. None came. She looked up. The crowd had silently stolen away.

At last, Jesus arose and asked, "Woman, where are your accusers? Has no man condemned you?"

Trembling, she stammered, "No man, Lord."

He looked into her eyes. "Neither do I condemn you: go, and sin no more." She stumbled

27

LIFE 101

away, weeping hot, healing tears that washed away her guilt and set her free. (Based on John 8.)

No matter what you have done, or how terrible
your sin, the Lord will forgive you
if you'll only repent and come to Him.

Day 3: *From Selflessness to Reward*

May the Lord repay you for what you have done.
May you be richly rewarded by the Lord. . . .
RUTH 2:12

Soon after Solomon was crowned king, two women came to him with babies, one dead, one living. The first said, "O king, we were sleeping with our children in one bed. This woman lay on her child in her sleep and it died. She put it beside me while I slept, took my baby, and said it was hers."

"She speaks falsely!" the other denied. "She is the mother of the dead child."

Solomon considered the problem for a long time. Then he said to a guard, "Take a sword, divide the living child, and give half to each woman."

One of the women said, "Yes. Cut the child in two and divide it between us." The other fell to her knees before the throne and cried out, "No, do not kill my son! Give the baby to her, but let him live."

Solomon ruled, "Give the child to the woman who would not have it slain. She is the real mother."

The woman who had been willing to give up her baby in order that he might live held the child close to her bosom and wept tears of joy. (Based on 1 Kings 3.)

Putting the interests of others ahead of our own brings great blessings.

LIFE 101

Day 4: *From Fear to Peace*

> *And the peace of God,*
> *which passeth all understanding,*
> *shall keep your hearts and minds*
> *through Christ Jesus.*
> PHILIPPIANS 4:7 KJV

Jesus knelt alone in the orchard of olive trees known as the Garden of Gethsemane. Peter, James, and John waited a little distance away, so weary they could not watch with Him even one hour. Soon Judas Iscariot would come with a band of men to seize Him. Now was the time to prepare for what lay ahead.

Great drops of sweat like blood fell to the earth. Groans wracked His tortured body and mind. One disciple had betrayed Him. Another would deny Him before the cock crowed in the morning. All would run away. Had those who followed learned so little in the weeks and months during which He had tried to teach them? The Son of God was also Son of man. The human side of Jesus shuddered. If only He could face death knowing His mission had not failed. Could those He had chosen carry on the work He had barely begun? Or would His sacrifice be for nothing?

"Father," He cried. "If it be possible, let this cup pass away from me. Nevertheless, not as I will, but as You will!" No sign came that God's plan would be altered. He bowed his head, so drained by the struggle, it felt as if life had flown, leaving only an empty shell.

Just when Jesus knew He could bear no more, an angel came from heaven and ministered to Him. A surge of peace flowed through Jesus.

Even though He watched his disciples vanish into the night, Jesus no longer feared. Weak and human as they were, in a short time their eyes would be opened. They would understand many things and serve Him until their deaths.

Heart and mind at peace, Jesus silently allowed his captors to lead him toward the high priest's house. (Based on Matthew 26; Luke 22.)

No matter how frightened or scared we are,
we can always find the peace that passes
understanding through Jesus Christ.

LIFE 101

I can do everything through him
who gives me strength.
PHILIPPIANS 4:13

Esther stood trembling outside the royal court. Dared she enter without invitation? If her husband, King Ahasuerus, did not hold out his golden scepter in welcome, she would be put to death. He had already banished Vashti, his former queen, for refusing to come at his command and show off her beauty to his drunken guests. What might he do to Esther for asking him to lift the death decree he had issued against the Jews?

"I cannot let my people be slaughtered," she whispered. "I am also Jewish. Should it be discovered, I will be subject to death. Besides, my people are counting on me." She gathered her royal robes about her and went into the inner court, heart pounding like the thunder of many chariots going to war.

When the king saw her, he held out the golden scepter and offered whatever she requested, up to half of his kingdom. Weak with relief, Esther invited him to a banquet, where she exposed the evil plotting of wicked Haman and saved her people from extermination. (Based on the Book of Esther.)

> Even when we feel too weak to meet
> tomorrow's challenges, we can ask for and
> receive strength from God.

Day 6: *From Oppression to Freedom*

Trust in the LORD with all thine heart; and lean not unto thine own understanding. In all thy ways acknowledge him, and he shall direct thy paths.
PROVERBS 3:5–6 KJV

Longer than many could remember, the children of Israel had been trapped in bondage by the Egyptians, who had made slaves of them.

At first they had clung to the promise of a

Deliverer, one who would lead them out of captivity. Yet as month after month dragged into long years of poverty, misery, and trouble, even that single ray of light in a dark world flickered low. "How long, O Lord?" the people cried out in despair.

God heard those cries. He saved Moses from Pharaoh's order that all boy babies born among the Jewish people must be killed and molded Moses to be a leader of the Israelites.

After many years of pleading and a series of terrible plagues, Pharaoh allowed Moses to lead the Exodus to the Promised Land. Gone were the people's hopelessness and helplessness. God Himself had freed them from oppression. (Based on Exodus 1–12.)

Patience and faith in the most difficult
circumstances will be rewarded.

Day 7: *From Anger to Understanding*

LIFE
101

*Love your enemies and pray for those
who persecute you. . .* MATTHEW 5:44

Simon Peter had never felt more miserable. How could Jesus allow this? Anger and hurt lay like stones in Peter's heart. His eyes flashed. "Even though all shall be offended, I will not," he declared. There! Now Jesus would know whatever happened, at least one would be beside Him. Jesus responded, "Peter, before the cock crows twice, you will deny me three times."

"If I should die with you, I will not deny you," he shouted. The others agreed.

A few hours later, Peter stared with consternation at Jesus. Had he not defended the Master by cutting off an enemy's ear with his own sword? Now it was back on the man's head as if it had never been severed! Why had Jesus healed one of those who came to take Him? Peter fled, confused and angry. By the second crowing of the cock the next morning, he had indeed denied Jesus three times.

Not until after Jesus' resurrection, did Peter begin to understand who and what Jesus really

LIFE 101

was. When he did, he gladly faced persecution, prison, and death rather than deny the Master. (Based on the Gospels of Matthew, Mark, Luke, and John.)

Placing yourself in another's shoes often turns anger to understanding.

Part 6

CLIFF NOTES

Before Jesus reached the mountain
where He taught and helped others,
He had to climb.

So do we!

LIFE 101

Bare Necessities to Help You Keep Climbing

✓ Life is not so much a destination as a journey.

✓ Start and end every day by giving your heavenly Father a "Thank You" for simply being alive.

✓ The way we choose to walk determines where we will end up.

✓ You will never fall as far if you're connected to a friend.

✓ There is always Someone who understands exactly how we feel.

✓ It's easier to recognize and avoid pitfalls by talking with someone who has already traveled that road.

✓ Jesus walked every path, felt every feeling, and overcame every obstacle we will ever have to face.

✓ When two walk together, the road never seems so long.

Others Who Will Often Walk with Us if only We Ask

✓ A dad, mom, or stepparent

✓ A sister or brother

✓ A relative outside the immediate family

✓ A neighbor

✓ A special friend

✓ A pastor, teacher, counselor, or doctor

✓ Most importantly, remember that you have a Friend in Jesus. You can always turn to Him in prayer.

My voice shalt thou hear
in the morning, O Lord;
in the morning will I direct
my prayer unto thee, and will look up.
Psalm 5:3 kjv

39

LIFE 101

Tomorrow

Beyond the shadows of a far distant shore;
The promises of tomorrow lie untouched in the
    mist,
Not quite reality—then again, much more,
Providing the reasons we exist.
The traces of days left behind grow silent, cease
    their whisperings.
Only faint memories remind of the joys and
    sorrows life brings.
With gaze ahead and heart behind, we lose the
    path on which we tread,
So intent we are to find the path that lies ahead.
And when the distant shore is reached,
When the day draws to a close,
The mists will lift and we will see
The joys of life were the paths we chose.